GOOD OL' RODEO DAYS

BILLY DEAN KLOEHR

teresa skinner publishing

Thanks to Jeremy Mangrum for making this book possible.

Copyright © 2019 by Linda Kloehr

All rights reserved.

No part of this book may be reproduced in any form or by any electronic or mechanical means, including information storage and retrieval systems, without written permission from the author, except for the use of brief quotations in a book review.

Print ISBN: 978-1-950123-40-7

Ebook ISBN: 978-1-950123-41-4

Published by Teresa Skinner Publishers

Cover Art Teresa Skinner

For my Family

Have you ever had one of those days you were glad you did not miss? My 32nd birthday, for the 48th time, or 80 years on this earth. With all of these beautiful children, grandchildren and great grandchildren around Mimi and Papa. The Lord had a hand in showing me Linda.

I will never have another 32nd birthday, from now on, they will be my 80th. There was so much love in the handwritten cards and letters. This old man still can't hold back the tears.

When I look back on my life, it was my Grandfather that put a mark on me. It is kinda funny, because all of this time because I thought I was bouncing off the walls of life. But it was Grandpa Stimple that taught me to talk to my Lord and listen to Him and His teachings. Even though you think you live right, there is always the thought, that I could have done better and then came this birthday.

I don't know how to say what is on my heart, so, I am going to say, "Thank you very much."
I love you all. Papa

Billy Dean Kloehr

Billy Dean Kloehr was born on September 20, 1935 in Coffeyville, Kansas to Lawrence "Earl" Kloehr and Inabelle "Susie" (Strimple) Kloehr. Billy was raised by his stepfather Frank Dix who instilled in him the many foundational building blocks that helped shape him into the man that he became. Shortly after graduating from Coffeyville High School in 1954 he raised his right hand and swore to defend the Constitution of the United States and joined the United States Air Force. Billy enlisted in the service on October 26, 1954 and honorably served our nation through August 25, 1958. He was not only a proud Air Force Veteran, but he was a very talented Pattern Maker and used that gifting to support his family for many years. Billy loved his family, especially his grandchildren and in his spare time he enjoyed fishing and being outdoors. He will always be remembered for his calm nature, strong character and loving spirit. Billy Dean Kloehr passed away on Thursday, June 20, 2019 in Tulsa, Oklahoma at the age of 83 while surrounded by his loving family.

Contents

How it All Started	1
Ricochet Rodeo	3
Frontier Days	7
The Runaways	11
Home Again	19

How it All Started

THE 1950'S WERE a good time for a kid to grow up. My name is Bill and I lived in a small town of Coffeyville, Kansas, in the Midwest. Growing up listening to radio, I think, gave me imagination to not be bored.

My mom's name was, Ina Bell, that's why they called her

Susie. She divorced my Dad years ago and remarried Frank. Frank was good to and for me. He taught me to hunt and to respect other people's property or at least he did his best.

Two other very special people were Jim and Delpha. They had a place ten miles north of town. Jim raised a few head of cows, some goats, and he had two horses. We met Jim at the fair and rodeo, where we all had aspirations of being the next Casey Tibbs, all-around champion cowboy.

This is the mix for this story of four kids who thought they were old enough to do most anything. We started going to Jim and Delpha's to ride horses and act like cowboys. At any one time there could be 10 to 20 kids at Jim and Delpha's. But the four of us Don, Leroy, Bob, and myself were the instigators of most of the goings on.

Ricochet Rodeo

ONE DAY, Jim said, "You know, they are having a small rodeo over by Caney, next Saturday. They will be riding Whiteface, if anyone is interested." Leroy was quick to say, "Hey, let's all go. I bet we could take all the prize money." I said, "How much is the entry fee?" "Well, I think it is a buck." Joe Luark said. "It was for guys your age." Meaning, fifteen to sixteen years of age. A dollar, was hard for me to come up with. But when I took my bike out after school and picked up bottles, I got enough to enter.

Bob and I made our ride pay off. Don and Leroy bucked off. Bob took first and I got second, and I made five bucks! Boy, I thought, "This is the way to make some money, you don't need a lot of schooling."

We rigged a barrel up on four cables, up about four feet off the ground. And then we put someone on it. We put two or three on each cable, to try to buck the rider off. We had seen a picture of Casey Tibbs doing this, in a magazine, only he had his over a swimming pool. We played at it hard and I guess helped us stay on the horse. For that summer we took in every rodeo that we could. I made more spending money than I ever had. However, my family had very little money so, it did not take much to be a lot.

One week, I was working north of town cutting, shocking and thrashing oats. When I got off work that night, Bob and I were in town. He said, "There is a rodeo over near Tyro, the entry is five bucks and we can get ten bucks, to exhibition a saddle bronc." "Well, we can't go wrong, the worst we can do is make five bucks," I said. So, that Saturday we headed out for Tyro.

Don couldn't make it that night but Leroy, Bob, Monty, and myself made it. Monty was from south town and was a hard luck guy. He rode bareback and looked good, but for some reason, he had few rides that went to the whistle. And that night was no different. Bob took second on bareback and I bucked off. But I took third in bull riding, which paid fifteen bucks. Then came the saddle bronc. Bob's went off without a hitch. However, everything went wrong with mine. To start with, the horse reared up as they opened the chute gate. Got his front legs over the gate, then settled down so much. as to stop dead in his tracks. Just outside the gate, I spurred as much as I could. It seemed like a long time, which was probably more like one second. Then he exploded! He went straight up, when he came down, I was still going up. This pulled me forward and down I came, only to meet a very solid saddle horn on its back up, in the middle of my chest. From then on, it was just hang on… until the pickup rider came by. The next day in the field, thrashing oats came very hard.

Bob had talked to Jim about building a rodeo arena on ten acres back of his barn and Jim said ok. So, we all started collecting as much cash as we could which was around twenty bucks. We took a trailer to the saw mill and spent all that we had on lumber. Next, we laid out the chutes and the catch pen. We all pitched in and by spring we were ready to go.

I remember Sunny, Bobs older brother, bought a horse at the sale barn. The man said he had never been ridden. Well, we thought he would give us some good experience in our new rodeo arena. The only problem, he would take two jumps out of the chute, then stop turn his head around and try to bite your leg. We all tried to ride him with the same results.

Then Bob got an idea. We put Ricochet, the name we gave the horse, in the chute. Then Bob got a tree limb about two inches round and two feet long. When the horse came out, he stopped and turned, as he had in the past. Bob came down between his ears with the club and the horse went down to the ground. When he came to, Bob was still on him. Ricochet never tried to bite him again as long as Sunny owned him.

Frontier Days

NOW, sometime later Sunny sold Ricochet because he needed the money. They were having a rodeo in Guthrie, Oklahoma, called Frontier Days. Sunny had entered in the bareback riding.

Bob and I had entered in the wild horse race. That's where they fill all of the chutes with horses and right after the National Anthem, they open all five chutes at the same time. Well, I picked out a horse with a long mane, because that's all you had to hold onto. When they finished with the anthem, I turned around to find a drunken cowboy on my horse, and the only horse left had a short mane. I got on just in time, they opened the gates, and away we went. The only thing I could see was that drunk cowboy on the ground, as my horse ran over him, I thought, "Good enough for ya."

Sunny got ready to ride his bareback when I heard him say, "Oh no, it's Ricochet." I didn't think we would get him down on that horse. He kept saying over and over, "He will bite me!" You see, Sunny was classified "four f" because of his nerves, and this had just done him in. Bob and I told him, "At least you know how he bucks." Well, Sunny rode him, but I don't remember him placing in the money.

Now came the highlight of the rodeo, if that is not enough. The drunken cowboy rode in the bull riding next. He drew one of the biggest bulls I had ever seen. The bull took him down the left side of the arena, and then, the cowboy was thrown over the bull's head, into a mud puddle. Then the bull then over him.

The drunk cowboy came back to the chutes, covered with mud, and he had blood all over his face. He yelled at the announcer, "Hey, I think he broke my leg." The announcer said, "Get to the ambulance behind the chutes." The cowboy limped around back to the ambulance, sure 'nuff, his leg was broken. Now, I felt sorry for him.

Now, with our new arena, all we needed was rodeo stock. We checked around and stock would cost seventy-five dollars. Here we go again, we took in every rodeo we could. We picked up bottles, we mowed lawns. But somehow, we came up with the money, so it was a go. We printed up flyers for the big day and put them up all over town. We had worked hard and decided to have a wiener roast and celebrate. We got our girlfriends, and that night, in a dry creek bed, we built a bonfire. Bob and Sunny, Bobs older brother, played guitars and we sang songs. We roasted wieners and marshmallows, until it started to rain. We all ran for the house. Bless her heart, Delpha let us in her small living room. There must have been twenty kids, wet of course. Delpha joined in and seemed to have as much fun as the rest of us.

I remember one time I had spent the night at Jim and Delpha's. I had gone hunting in the morning. I could eat most anything. Well this day, I had shot an opossum, and my mom would not cook anything like that. So, I asked Delpha. She said, "Yes, but I'm not going to eat any and you will have to." I said, "I will try it. But, if it's not any good, I won't eat it, ok?" Delpha agreed. Well, I remember opening the oven and theses white ribs standing in a pool of grease, with very little meat visible. I took one bite and that was all I could eat.

In the morning after the wiener roast, we headed back to the farm. It was the only rodeo and none of us wanted to be late. When we got there, we found we had another problem. You see Jim's place set on top of a hill, and with the rain the night before, the stock trucks were half way up the hill, with Jim's tractor and seven kids who had worked so hard to put this show on. We got the trucks up and unloaded.

Some of the girls took the money at the gate, the rest of us parked cars and ran concession. We must have had sixty or seventy cars, with pop and candy sales. We might have broken even if we were lucky.

We were not so lucky in the arena. In the past, Leroy had a hard time holding onto his bull rope, so he tied his hand in and when the bull tossed him, he couldn't let go. Well, that bull might still be dragging him around if his hand had not come out of his glove. We still had a hard time getting the rope off the bull.

I had a steer set up on me and like to got a horn in my gut. Bob's horse ran over a calf in the calf roping and broke the calf's leg. It was Jim's calf, so we butchered it when the show was all over, and we were sitting around most of us banged up but nothing.

Jim said "Well you guys put on one hell of a show but half of the time you sacred me stiff. Now, I know your folks probably do not care if you are out here having fun, but if one of you got hurt bad, your folks might take a dim view of me letting you ride horses and bulls out here. So, I am asking you to get written permission. I know you have put in a lot of work, but I have also had a lot invested in this place and I could lose it all." Bob said, "You know he is right Leroy, you could have a broken arm. Bill, you could have a whole in your gut. Hell, we could all be busted up." "Jim's right, I know it might be hard to get folks to sign." I said, "But I know if it was my place, you would have had permission before this show." We all agreed to try to get our parents to sign a release.

Well, to make a long story short, you guessed it, no one got a released signed. Now, we were in our last of high school, but we decided that this had more importance than book learning. After all, this what we were going to do the rest of our lives. Well, at least that is what we thought, so, what do we do about it? We had no money, so we could not start over. And if we could where?

The Runaways

Chaps bought from rodeo money

I AM NOT real sure how we all came up with the answer to run away from home. Maybe with young people like we were, when we felt like we were painted into a corner, that was the only thing we could do. At any rate this started a very nice adventure for the four of us.

Like I said, we were broke. Had no transportation, and no way to get any either. We needed some money for food, so we all tried to dig up as much as we could. I remembered I had put up a deposit of two dollars and eighty-five cents for a pair of safety glasses in my vocational machine shop. So, we decided to leave town Monday morning. We packed some clothes in a sack or box along with as much food as we thought would not be missed and hid them in the alley.

The next morning, we got up and went to school as normal. When I got to school, I told Ila Jean the girl, I was going with, that we were headed to Paris, Texas. The rest of the guys did the same with their girlfriends. When school opened, I went in and told the principle my family was moving to Texas for work. I could not believe how easy it was. I went around to my classes and checked out and in machine shop I turned in my safety glasses and got my deposit. This made me the richest one of the four.

Now, Darrel C. had a car but did not want to go with us, so we asked him to take the four of us out west where we could start hitchhiking. We got on the road somewhere around nine thirty. There was a wide spot in the road so, Darrel pulled over. We started getting out and Leroy said, "Here comes a car." Don said, "Stick out your thumb." Well as soon the car started to stop, we all grabbed our sacks or boxes and started to run, to where Leroy was. When the driver saw us coming, he gave it the gas and took off.

"Lesson number one," I said. "We will have to split up or no one will give us a ride. Let's flip to see who hikes together." We agreed Bob and Don went first. Pratt would be or first meeting place, unless we got a ride to Garden City. Yes, we were not going to Paris, Texas, as we told all the girls. We were headed for

Good Ol' Rodeo Days

Cheyenne, Wyoming. Why? Well the only thing that was mentioned was Cheyenne Frontier Days, which was a long way off. We thought we would get jobs until the rodeo started. We pick small towns to meet so, it would not be hard to find the other two and this worked very well. We were never separated for more than four or five hours.

We spent the first night under a bridge in Great Bend, Kansas, and it was cold. One good thing about that is we were up and ready to go early. Bob and Don took off first and got a ride right off. But Leroy and I were at least an hour waiting for a ride.

We had such a hard time that Leroy and I split up. I recall one ride with an old gentleman. When he stopped, I ran to get into the car and he said, "Would you get that pop bottle please?" As he pointed to the side of the road, I said "Sure." When I go back to the car he said, "Put it in the back." When I looked in the back it was covered with pop bottles. He went about twenty yards and stopped again and said, "There's another one," as he pointed to the ditch. This went on for fifteen miles and lasted longer and cost me more in getting out and picking up bottles than almost any ride we have taken to Wyoming. I think I could have walked and made better time. We had agreed to meet in north Platte that night.

Well, Leroy and I teamed back up and we got a ride with two drunks. I was so, so glad to get to north Platte. Phil and Windle. Phil was driving, or at most he had his hands on the steering wheel, most of the time Windle would yell at Phil when he got on the left-hand side of the road and a car was coming. Phil would whip the car back on the right side of the road and yell at Windle, "Well I was trying to miss that rock on the shoulder back there." Windle said, "Well hell, man you almost hit that car." Phil said, "I just wanted to see if you were awake. Give me another drink." It went on like that for sixty miles.

We stopped at a service station sometime after sundown. Bob and Don were there so, we told Phil this was as far as we were going and thanked them for the ride. They pulled out of the station and hit the curb on the other side of the road before getting straightened out and headed into town. We never saw them again. I told Bob "I was never so glad to get out of a car in all of my life."

The owner of the station had some old cars out back and said we could sleep in, so I went and crashed for about thirty minutes.

I woke up to Don shaking me saying, "Come on Bill, we have a ride all of the way to Cheyenne." I got up and went out front. The ride was a pickup so, that meant two in the front and two in the back the guy had a V8 motor in the back with a tarp over it. Don and I jumped in the back, one on either side of the motor. We tried to cover up with the tarp at sixty or seventy miles per hour. There was not much that helped. We like to have froze to death, but we held together.

When we got to Cheyenne, we took five dollars and had Leroy go into this old hotel and rent a room. The rest of us slipped up to the room after the lady went back to her room. In the room, we got to talking about the trip and got to have laughing so hard and loud that the lady came back and knocked on the door and said, "How many are in there? Come on out." We gathered our stuff up and one by one walked out she looked back in the room and said, "Any more in there?" With all heads hanging, Leroy said, "No ma'am that's all, we are sorry for making so much noise." She cut us a little slack, "If you get out now, I will not call the law." We left right away.

By this time, it was 1AM. Two things, we needed a place to stay and we needed a job. We found the unemployment office. From there we walked to the rodeo area thinking we could find a place to sleep. The only door that was open was to the restroom, we went in and tried to bed down. The concrete was hard, but it was cold, so, we tried to build a fire to keep warm. The smoke was so bad, we had to put it out and abandon that idea.

Now, we are looking at 5AM. I said, "I am going back to the unemployment office and wait for it to open." Don said, "OK, let's go to the bus station first, we can put our bags in one of those lockers, that way, if we find work, we will be ready to go." "Good idea, let's go."

So, that is how we came to be the first in line at the unemployment office. When this man came in and said I need five men to dig ditches. The four of us, plus the man behind us got the job. They were putting in a new television station out east of town ad inside they were putting air conditioning in the ground. Our job was to dig ditches for the duct work. The ground was so hard, we had to use picks to break it up. We told everyone that we were eighteen. This was October, I was the only one that was eighteen, by almost one month.

There was a lot of construction work going on in the building and the men doing the work were great. They did a lot of teasing. Like the time we were digging a ditch up to this wall. The ground level on the other side of the wall was eight feet lower, the duct work had to go under the wall. But we didn't know that, Some of the men had dug the ditch under the other side so, when we dug down far enough the ground gave way, and down Bob and I went, with Don and Leroy not that far behind. It was all in good clean fun, and we all had a big laugh.

We asked the boss if we could have an advance on our wages, he gave us twenty bucks each. Boy, that made us feel a lot better, now we could eat a lot better. We sent Leroy into the Wyoming hotel to rent a room. The place had a side door that was locked from the outside, so, Leroy came down and opened it and in we went.

This time no funny stuff. We even cleaned the place up before going to work. Here we go, down to the bus station, every morning before breakfast, with our sacks over our shoulder to put them in the locker. Get the key, go to eat breakfast, then off to work.

Well, on the fifth day, in the bus station, a large man in a suit walked up to me and said, "How old are you?" I turned and said, "Eighteen, why?" He didn't answer me, he turned to Leroy and asked, "Does your Mother know where you are?" Leroy said, "Yes." The man said, "Let' call her." I think we all knew without asking, that this guy was the law because Leroy said nothing. He just went to pay the phone, he picked up the phone and the man put a dime in it. Leroy dialed the number. We were had.

The man took the receiver and asked, "Do you know where your boy is?" He pulled out a pad and started writing. Then, he hung the phone up and turned to us and said, "Let's go to the station, you are being charged with runaway and vagrancy." He took us downtown and booked us. One call was to our boss to let him know we would not be to work. We were fingerprinted, had mug shots made and place two in a cell.

The next day we had to go to court. The judge read the charges and asked, "How do you plead?" Bob spoke up, "Judge we are not vagrants, we have jobs out at the new television station and we are staying at the best hotel in town." He didn't tell him that only one was paying for the room. The judge didn't know, so he dropped the charge of vagrancy. He did hold us on the charge of run away until our folks could send the money to come home. I think by this time; we could have used our own money to get home. Although, we were having a good time until that lawman came into the picture.

The money came and one of the policemen took us to the bus station and bought our tickets. We asked him if he would take us to get our checks, and he did. The guys at work really laid it on us. We got our checks and said our goodbyes. The police took us back to the bus station. He said, "I am going to leave you guys, now, be sure you do not miss your bus, or I will have to put you back in jail." We assured him we would be on the bus. When we left, there was a western store across the street, so, we walked over and went to look around. We each had about thirty bucks, that was just burning a hole in our pockets. What better place to spend it. I do not remember what anyone else bought, but I walked out with a brand-new pair of chaps.

The bus came and we got on. There were six or seven guys on the bus, and the further the bus went, the drunker they got. We could not understand, because there was no booze sold in Cheyenne. We were singing with them and having a good time, when one handed me a bottle of after shave. I said, "No thanks." And he tipped it up and drank it.

Boy! These guys would drink anything, and being in a dry state, or unable to get booze, did not stop them.

Home Again

BACK HOME, I was surprised my folks did not beat the tar out of me. As a matter of fact, they treated me rather well. Frank said he would sign a release, if I wanted this bad. He did and said be careful. I think it was mom that did not want me to rodeo.

Back at school, it was a different story. We all had to go in and see the principle. He did not want us back in school, he let us know in so many words. It may have been, the ol' boy was just that smart. Because, we all said, you cannot keep us out of school. We will be here every day and we are going to graduate. He stopped for a second, then looked us square in the eye, one by one, and said, "If you give me one reason to expel you, you are out of here so fast your head will spin. Now if all of you agree, get to class now." We did not have to talk it over. We were out of there. Someone said that he took off six percent for each day we were gone. Six days adds up to thirty-six percent. I do not know about that, my grades were bad enough, but we did graduate. Maybe because he did not want us back for another year.

We made some rodeos after that, some of us, more than others. But none of us were destined to take Casey Tibbs place in history. Leroy was killed in a car wreck some years later. Sunny, died about fifteen years ago. Don, last I heard, working for a manufacturing company. Bob called a few weeks ago and declared his retirement. Jim died, around the time that Sunny passed away. Delpha and her daughter, Norma come by my shop in Wagoner about ten years ago. They both looked good. Norma started a pig farm, I understand that she is shipping all over the world, or maybe just part of it. I went into business for my self 20 years ago. I have lost track of the rest of the bunch. Maybe Bob can fill in some.

Forty five years later, I still have the chaps I bought in Cheyenne. They are well used, and the leather is coming apart. But, they are still a reminder of the "Good Old Days"

Printed July 10, 2019

www.ingramcontent.com/pod-product-compliance
Lightning Source LLC
Chambersburg PA
CBHW020121130526
44591CB00031B/276